Terms and Conditions

LEGAL NOTICE

The Publisher has strived to be as accurate and complete as possible in the creation of this report, notwithstanding the fact that he does not warrant or represent at any time that the contents within are accurate due to the rapidly changing nature of the Internet.

While all attempts have been made to verify information provided in this publication, the Publisher assumes no responsibility for errors, omissions, or contrary interpretation of the subject matter herein. Any perceived slights of specific persons, peoples, or organizations are unintentional.

In practical advice books, like anything else in life, there are no guarantees of income made. Readers are cautioned to reply on their own judgment about their individual circumstances to act accordingly.

This book is not intended for use as a source of legal, business, accounting or financial advice. All readers are advised to seek services of competent professionals in legal, business, accounting and finance fields.

You are encouraged to print this book for easy reading.

Table Of Contents

Foreword

Chapter 1:
The Benefits Of Membership Sites

Chapter 2:
What Kind Of Site To Make

Chapter 3:
Background On Using Word Press To Set Up TheSite

Chapter 4:
wp-Member

Chapter 5:
Using Clickbank For Payment Processing

Wrapping Up

Foreword

If the word 'product' is mentioned, individuals instantly think 'eBook' – all the same, this isn't always the case. You may do an audio product, a custom made software package, a produced script that does things differently or even a membership site.

The beauty of your own products is that you build up a reputation – regardless what niche you're in, if you demonstrate yourself to produce quality, individuals will purchase from you. Over again and again and again and once again.

You likewise have the option of enrolling a horde of affiliates to distribute your products, something you don't have the choice of as an affiliate (unless there are 2 tiers... but few chances like this exist these days). Get a great product with raging testimonials and a slayer sales page (all of which may be outsourced), contact a few of the big shots in your niche... and bang, you're making cash.

Naturally, the issue with using your own products compared to affiliate marketing... is that you have to produce the product yourself, but we can show you how.

How To Create A Membership Website To Sell On Clickbank

Chapter 1:
The Benefits Of Membership Sites

Synopsis

If you've been paying attention to the hum surrounding the subject of membership sites on the Net, you'll have heard about the numerous advantages of owning one. On the other hand, if you're new to the concept, you might be wondering what the huge deal is.

In this chapter, we'll go over 5 of the advantages to owning a membership site. These benefits can be passed along to buyers of your product.

The Advantages

Passive revenue: The beginning and most obvious advantage of any membership site is the passive revenue it returns from membership fees. The definition of passive revenue is "revenue derived from investments in which the individual is minimally involved." To be successful, a solid first effort is required to get your site running and a passive revenue stream running. After that, you might well discover yourself bringing in more and working less.

With a passive revenue, you are able to make money 24/7. Contrary to a service based business, with a business that returns passive revenue, you are able to take your loved ones on vacation and still make revenue while you're away from the office.

Residual revenue: Membership sites likewise enable you to bring in residual revenue. Residual revenue is revenue that keeps coming in to you on a steady basis. When you produce a membership site, your buyer will be paying a monthly membership fee for a period of time that you assign.

You might only charge your buyers 12 payments, and after they've paid those payments, grant them a life membership at no further cost. You might opt to charge an annual renewal fee, or you might decide to have the payments billed to them on a continual monthly basis for as long as they stay a client. Whichever technique you pick out, you're producing residual revenue for yourself.

Cheap to begin: a different awesome benefit to a membership site is that it's relatively cheap to begin. naturally you'll need to put some cash into it, but if you are able to do the web design work yourself and

decide to market your business utilizing free marketing techniques, you are able to get your site up and running for little money. That includes the domain registration, hosting account, membership management platform, and any other tools like an auto responder.

Authority position: As your membership grows in fame, so will your reputation. You'll start to be seen as an authority in your field. Subscribers will look to you for advice and inherently trust your discernment. Basically, you'll be constructing and marketing your own brand. When you have a recognized and entrusted brand, you dramatically step-up your power to provide other products and services under that same brand. As your brand is tested and trusted, your fresh products automatically become trusted too.

Integral affiliates: By providing an affiliate plan, your buyers will be able to bring in revenue by the referrals they bring to you. If you're constantly providing your buyers excellent content and quality info, they'll most likely be happy to tell other people about your site; couple that with the fact that they may bring in money doing that, and they'll be shouting your praises from the rooftops.

When the bulk of your buyers are helping you to promote your membership site, you'll be able to reach a much higher number of likely buyers than you would ever be able to grasp through your solo promotion efforts. This, naturally, will lead to a higher number of new subscribers and a higher income.

These are simply a couple of the advantages associated with owning a membership site. These as well are benefits you can let you buyers know about to get them interested in your membership site product.

Chapter 2:
What Kind Of Site To Make

Synopsis

Bunches of membership sites fail miserably. Bunches bring in tens or hundreds of thousands of dollars monthly. If you wish to succeed in putting together sites that will sell I advocate that you take notes and answer the crucial questions as we continue.

Choose The Niche

Explore

This is the step that distinguishes the winners from the losers (financially wise) yet it's the step that you'll be most disposed to sail through. You'll feel the itch to skip ahead to producing a site, a logo or a product as that's the fun part. Suitable research before getting rolling will determine the success or failure of your product.

Here are the queries you have to research and how you are able to research them:

Who's your membership site is going to assist?

Specifying your target market is square one and you likely already have it in mind. Most individuals answer this question too loosely. You have to dig down your target market to discover a niche in the market. Attempting to please everyone is the easiest way to fail!

Is there a particular part of the process that your market is clambering with? Is there a particular niche of individuals inside your market that you may center on? These are awesome questions you are able to utilize to help you discover a niche inside the market that you already have in mind.

Does the market or niche you've selected have a big frustrating issue that they need worked out?

You need to assess the level of frustration that the individuals are experiencing in the niche before getting moving. The greater the

frustration, the more likely they'll be searching for your info and pay for access to your info and product.

To ascertain the level of frustration in your niche do not simply visit the Google Keyword Tool to see how many searches there are monthly. Most gurus will tell you to do the Keyword Tool may be misleading for estimating a need. There are lots of niches that do numerous searches that don't really have that big of a need.

A great example is dog owners that can't get their dogs to stop barking. The term "stop dog barking" gets 90,500 searches per month on Google. This would make you think there is a huge painful problem because there are so many people searching. The reality is that most people are just passively annoyed. Their need isn't big enough to warrant paying for a solution.

If the Google Keyword Tool isn't that valuable in determining the level of a frustration, issue or need, how may you learn?

Message bulletin boards, Yahoo Answers and blog comments on related matters to your niche are awesome ways to discover what sort of questions are being asked. If much of the same questions are being asked and there's frustration in the questions then there's a large painful issue that your membership site may solve.

A different awesome way to ascertain if there's a big frustrating urgent need is to see how much rivalry there is and if they're making revenue.

If there's much rivalry and you discover that they're making revenue this shows there's a large need in the market.

View Google Adwords (the sponsored advertisements on the right of Google). If there are a lot of the same advertisements over time that's a big sign. Companies wouldn't be spending cash on ads for months at a time if they weren't bringing in any cash.

You are able to likewise email other site owners in the market to learn! Successful rivalry is a beautiful thing because it implies that there the need in the niche is so large that multiple companies have to fill it!

This is the most crucial part of researching for your membership site. Don't go all out with your first idea. You have to be cutthroat! If there isn't a big frustrating issue, discover a different market or niche that has a big, frustrating issue that you are able to solve!

What are the particular issues that your niche is baffled with?

You are an awesome example. You aren't really baffled by beginning a net business; you're baffled or confused about setting up membership sites, picking out a payment processor, producing content, shipping options and/or other particular issues.

Discover the particular issues that individuals are having troubles with and center your membership and its material around this.

To discover this, the best way is to get in the ditches and speak with people.

If you have an e-mail list, surveying is an awesome way to discover these tiny things that your niche needs help with. Ask a couple of

questions like "What piece of [the issue they're experiencing] is inducing you the most frustration?" You'll receive an entire list of responses.

I advise that you take each of these responses and make the key topic (frustration) from everyone a bullet on a line of a page. Write it out by hand so that you'll truly take in the answers.

What you'll have in the end is a list of issues that individuals are baffled with. These bullet points then become the material for your membership site. It's that easy!

How is your web site going to be unlike the other membership sites out there?

In niches that have big baffling needs there's commonly a lot of rivalry. Some of this rivalry will to be sure utilize a membership site. Why will individuals in the niche select your membership product over a different membership site or product? What makes your site and your offer dissimilar?

Perhaps you're what makes your membership different as you've an incredible story or a ridiculous amount of believability. Perhaps you center in on one particular topic inside your niche.

You have to discover an unparalleled marketing suggestion. How are you going to stick out in your market in a way that will make individuals in the niche choose your product?

If you don't stick out in a particular place in the visitor's brains, they won't purchase your product no matter how unbelievable the material is!

How will you get to be an expert?

Nobody will purchase from you unless you base yourself as an expert.

If individuals see you as the best in your industry, they'll seek you out, purchase your product and pay more for it!

How do you base yourself as the finest?

Social substantiation.

How may you connect and basically utilize the top players in your industry to establish your social substantiation? This may be as easy as getting photos with gurus in your field or having them mail their list advocating your products.

Become originative. There are lots of assorted ways to establish yourself as being the finest in your niche. It's crucial that you figure this out before you get moving.

Chapter 3:
Background On Using Word Press To Set Up The Site

Synopsis

There isn't a deficit of ways to construct membership / subscription based sites with WordPress. Of course the first things you need are a place to host the site, a URL that will grab search engine attention and for the purposes of this book, Word Press installed. If you don't know how to install Word Press, look for a host that has Fantastico for an easy install.

The following thing you require for producing your membership site with WordPress is a great theme. They're a few different WordPress theme developers that supply very flexible and highly customizable themes, some paid and some free.

The First Steps

Your site's look is decided by your theme. A great theme will make the difference between a professional-looking web site and one that isn't.

You ought to pick out your theme straightaway, as it does have an effect on how you produce your content (that is., two or three-column layouts, screen width, and so forth). In WordPress, content is generally separate from presentation, so you are able to always alter your theme later.

If you do this though you'll lose most of the work that you've put into tailor-making your theme, so it's better to begin right away with the theme that you'll be finally utilizing.

Themes are customizable to differing levels. All themes may be customized by altering the PHP theme files, but this may be technical and time-consuming. You're better off picking a theme that already has the functionality and the feel that you need.

You're likewise generally better off picking a Theme framework over a regular theme. This will be described further. A theme framework lets you customize options like the presence or absence of side-bars with the theme options page.

Here is how I get going:

Begin with WordPress most popular (free) themes (http://wordpress.org/extend/themes/browse/popular/) – you might discover a "home run" theme there, and if not you may acquire

a few ideas. Recall that there are disadvantages to utilizing a regular theme vs. a theme framework, even if that theme is a "home run" from a visual viewpoint.

Think about Artisteer. This is a Windows software package that you are able to design the layout locally and has a lot of assorted options. When you're done you export the theme files and upload to your web site with FTP. It produces visually rich sites, although a bit on the simple side. Likewise works for Joomla and Drupal CMS.

All the same, recommended Theme frameworks:
- Atahualpa (gratis, install from your WP Dashboard)
- Thesis
- Studio Press
- iThemes Builder or Flexx

The reason a theme framework is advocated, is that most anything that you wish to do later you'll be able to do thru customizing the theme options inside your dashboard, instead of modifying the theme files in PHP.

Remember: you are able to do almost anything you wish with WordPress – all the same it will be more or less work depending upon whether your theme supports it (and/or whether you are able to discover a plug-in that supports it).

Choice of support is likewise a serious worry. In numerous cases paid themes supply better support. The exclusion to this is Atahualpa.

Hybrid, WhiteHouse, Lysa and Thematic. These all install directly from your WP dashboard and have a clean uncluttered look and are free.

A couple of good paid ones you might want to check out include WooThemes, StudioPress, ElegantThemes and SoloStream. They can be used for a lot of different projects. SoloStream specifically makes really plain looking themes that don't have a lot of graphic elements to them but a lot of framework.

This makes the themes extremely customizable for users that are to a greater extent web design inclined. If you're not a designer and don't have the time to learn all of that stuff then WooThemes, StudioPress, and ElegantThemes are better options.

Decide if you're going to require drop-down menus, as not all themes support them. If you've less than ten pages on your site, don't utilize drop-down menus.

If you're seeking a theme for a particular niche, try searching the WordPress theme directory site or Google for that particular keyword theme.

If you buy a commercial theme, you'll have to upload it to your site and activate it. The simplest way to do this is thru the appearance > theme > add new theme choices (WordPress dashboard), then use the "Upload" tab, and navigate to the theme zip file supplied by your theme vendor.

The 2nd way to this is to unzip the theme then upload it thru FTP. You'll require an FTP client software for this, and you'll need to know your hosting account username and password.

How to alter a theme

The initial thing you'll commonly do is replace the banner and logo. You are able to make yourself a banner utilizing free image editing software. You'll have to upload your banner picture to your site utilizing FTP, and place it inside the right directory of your server (commonly ./wp-content/themes/yourthemename/images).

The dearest themes and theme frameworks likewise give you control of the styling of each element of your web site, like background color, font, margins, and so on. You have to know a little CSS to accomplish this, but this is really simple and you are able to Google "CSS background color" (or whatever) for the exact instructions.

One you've styled your site to your desired look-and-feel, you have to setup your side-bars. You can do this with Widgets.

- In WordPress admin go to Appearance > Widgets
- Choose the left or right side-bar (on the far right screen)
- Drag your selection onto the side-bar and edit it / tailor-make it.
- Save your settings, then look at your site

The most crucial widget to understand is the "Text" widget, which lets you put in customized html text to your side-bar.

WordPress Membership Plug-in

So you have got your theme put together, now let's go into the meat of what you require for your membership site, a membership plug-in.

You can look through lists of plug-ins to decide which one is for you or you are able to just go with wp-Member, issue resolved. The main reason for its fame is due to its API and 3rd party extensions that make it simple to tailor-make for any sort of membership site you wish to build.

The most crucial features that applies to everybody is that it's compatible with a lot of different payment processors like Clickbank, PayPal, 1ShoppingCart and more. You are able to produce unlimited membership levels and you are able to protect each part of your WordPress site.

Make sure to always test the site.

Chapter 4:
wp-Member

Synopsis

wp-Member is an advanced WordPress membership plug-in that imparts a lot of membership features.

To Get The Payments For The Site

Web site owners may alter login/registration background graphic and font colors on login/registration page.

Add customized registration fields .Drag and Drop areas to alter field order on registration form.

Every post, page and category may have one or more membership levels allotted, allowing access to members who have the right membership level. If you are able to place it on a WordPress post, page or category, wp-Member may easily protect it with one click.

The members will solely be able to view material if their subscription includes the membership level which the material they're attempting to view is assigned to. Members won't be able to view content assigned to additional membership levels.

Conceal blocks of content inside posts and pages from unregistered members. Paragon for supplying teasers, or hiding the end of the post or page so that people must login or register to be able to see the remainder of the material.

Members who aren't registered will see a message in place of the concealed material. You are able to edit this message to state anything that you like a call to action informing the buyer that they have to register or login before they may see the content. You are able to even include html.

Each member's account will be mechanically managed so that owners don't have to do anything. As soon as a member signs up, their account will be mechanically produced. If the member's subscription

calls for a payment, the member will be directed to their selected payment method. Till the members payment has been substantiated, their account will stay inactive and if they attempt to login, they'll be asked to conclude their payment before their account will be triggered and they'll be able to see secure material.

Once the member's payment has been confirmed, their account will be automatically activated and they will then be able to login and access the content assigned to their membership level.

If a member calls off their subscription or is late creating a payment, their account will be frozen till they bring their payments up to date. Once the member attempts to login, they'll be shown payment choices so that they may update their payment. When their account has obtained a substantiated payment, their account will be mechanically unsuspended and they'll be able to login and get at the material specified to their membership level.

wp-Member goes with gateway modules for PayPal, Authorize.net and Google Checkout. It's up to you which gateways you wish to utilize for the site. You are able to utilize no gateways (if you don't want to charge for the membership plans), or any mixture of gateways. Your users will be able to choose which gateway they would prefer to utilize when they register.

You are able to produce unlimited membership levels and specify to each membership level as few or as many posts, pages and classes as you want. Every level may have unlimited subscriptions. Subscriptions may be set to repeating payments, or one off payments, each with a length from payment to the next of one day to ninety-nine years!

If dealing with buyers payments, you have to ensure that your software can't be hacked; otherwise a hacker may add malicious code to the payment procedure in an attempt to steal your buyer's particulars, perpetrate identity theft or fraud.

This is something that you need to prevent totally. wp-Member utilizes the latest encryption techniques making it utterly impossible for anybody to be able to hack or differently change your payment process. This supplies both the site owner and all the buyers with the best possible security and serenity.

A: wp-Member does not interfere with your theme settings. As such, it will not cause any conflicts with correctly coded themes. The only themes that we have ever found which caused issues when used with wp-Member included incorrect coding when managing ajax features on the admin side. As such, these themes simply needed to be corrected so that they did not cause problems caused by incorrect coding.

wp-Member works closely with the existing WordPress user scheme so that web site admins may manipulate the site to fit their needs.

Only membership levels that bear subscriptions assigned to them will be useable for users to choose when registering on the WordPress website. An admin will be able to manually add selected users to the obscured membership levels. This may be utilized to give selected users bonuses that are unavailable to additional users, or if you needed to provide selected material that related only to the member you promoted to the concealed membership level.

Always test the site.

Chapter 5:
Using Clickbank For Payment Processing

Synopsis

Clickbank repeating billing is a fully automated scheme that makes marketing, promoting, and handling recurring transactions simple and profitable. Clickbank recurring billing subscriptions supply you with the flexibleness to sell and market a wide array of products and services.

Utilizing A Different Method

Subscriptions let you sell and promote products and services, like software licenses and membership sites, in which buyers get ongoing value. Clickbank repeating billing subscriptions let you tailor-make your regularly scheduled buyer payments with features like:

- The power to have a lower first price
- The power to provide a test period
- The power to choose from new rebilling frequency choices

The power to set a lower first price gives you flexibleness when designing your recurring billing product or service, as owners are able to increase the payment for subsequent rebills.

A test period lets you offer your buyers a short time period to try the membership site at a reduced price before the regularly scheduled payments start.

With rebilling frequency choices, you are able to select bi-weekly, every month, quarterly, and yearly billing. With these flexible choices, you are able to offer a bigger assortment of products and services in the market.

Producing a recurring billing, subscription, or membership product is similar to making a standard product, but with a couple of unique steps.

Please cautiously check that all info about your product is correct before submitting it for approval, as repeating billing products can't be altered once they're approved.

To produce a recurring billing product, take the accompanying steps:

- Travel to My Account and log in to your Clickbank account.
- Click Account Settings.
- Click My Products.
- Click Recurring Billing Products.
- Click Add New Product.
- Add the essential information to the Adding a Product window.
- Click Save Changes.
- The system will specify a status of Approval Request Required to the product.

Pose a test buy:

- Click My Site under Account Settings.
- In the Testing Your Products box, click on Generate New Card Number.
- This will produce a charge card number, expiration date, and validation code you are able to utilize to pose test orders. This card data will be valid for 24 hours, after which time it will run out and will no more be available for test orders.
- Observe the charge card info.
- Go to the Pitch Page for the product you wish to test, and click through the payment link, which ought to take you to the Clickbank order form.
- Enter data into every field of the order form. You are able to utilize any address data you wish, but enter the test charge card details you produced.

- Affirm the data on the order confirmation page. Click through to download your product, which ought to take you to the right Thank You Page URL for the product you're trying out.

Petition product approval by clicking on Request Approval in the action column of the recurring billing product list.

Fill in the Request Product Approval form.

- Affirm the info and provide extra information if necessary.
- Click on Submit Product Approval Request at the bottom of the form. Make certain all data is right before clicking on Submit, as your product can't be altered once it's approved.
- The scheme will assign a condition of Approval Requested.
- A team member from the Clickbank product approval department will go over your site and product info to determine if it will be Okayed or rejected as a recurring billing product.
- If Okayed, the system will update the product condition to Approved.
- If rejected, the system will update the product status to Disapproved.
- Your repeating billing product is now live and ready to sell!

Unlike a lot of the competitors, Clickbank doesn't quit after one payment failure. Clickbank realizes that scheduled payments might fail for many reasons, including insufficient funds, so they have optimized their recurring billing process to decrease authorization declines and increase revenue.

In the event that buyers' charge card can't support the payment request, they'll attempt authorization again 3 days after the 1ST failure date. After a 2nd failure, they'll reattempt 4 days after the 2nd failure date. After a 3rd failure, they'll try once more 7 days after the 3rd failure date. A 4th failure will lead to an automatic cancellation of the subscription purchase. They send notifications to the buyer and vendor on the final 2 attempts.

For subscriptions the rebill sum may be bigger than the initial payment amount. The lower limit initial price is $4.95, and the lower limit rebill price is $7.95.

Remember though that you can't alter the initial, or rebill price for any recurring billing product once it has been Okayed by the product approval team. If someone wants to alter the initial, or re-bill price of a product for future sales, they'll need to produce a new product in the My Products section of the account. This is one of the drawbacks to using Clickbank for your product.

Wrapping Up

If you're seeking a fresh product to offer your buyers and prospects or you would like to produce a new revenue current, think about adding a membership web site to your current business model. A membership site provides a ton of huge business building advantages including that you need to point out to potential product buyers:

Expanded income – a membership may easily get to be among the most valued and frequently bought products. In and of itself, recurring membership renewals may provide a uniform flow of money and expanded profits. Suppose that 10% of someone's present subscribers signed up for their membership site at a fee of ten dollars per month (naturally individuals likely charge more than this.) Adding it up, that means a uniform flow of revenue and a step-up in someone's monthly income.

Step-up site traffic – membership sites by their nature involve visits to a site which single handedly step-ups site traffic. All the same, as well as member visits someone will likely also step-up visits to their site through marketing efforts and word of mouth. Individuals love membership sites and if a free membership level is offered people will draw an enormous amount of fresh traffic to the site.

Remain in contact with buyers and leads – memberships, whether gratis or paid, provide business owners yet a different way to remain in touch with their leads and buyers. Frequent communication is among the keys to increasing a client base, allegiance, brand awareness, and earnings.

Send out special offers for added sales – a membership site supplies people with the unparalleled opportunity to communicate particular offers to their prospects thru their membership interface. This steps up their opportunity for added sales. These may be sales of his own products, affiliate sales, or joint venture partnership opportunities.

Provide faithful buyers and members coupons, perks and discounts so they spend a lot. A membership site gives owners the chance to reward allegiance by supplying a forum or tool to share coupons, particular promotions, discounts and additional loyalty driven offers. Allegiance marketing has been demonstrated to step-up earnings.

Provide expanded value to current buyers – the customer, after all, is what it's all about, correct? A membership site supplies owners with the chance to better the value to their buyer by offering them one more product or source of info.

Fortify their brand – their own membership site supplies them with the chance to beef up their brand. Membership sites, spread information, may be really search engine friendly, generate buzz, are frequented often and help an owner construct a community around their business. All of these help beef up their brand.

Membership sites provide the owner a really unique and potentially fruitful way to grow their existing business. Once again, I advocate utilizing the WordPress platform with wp-member as your membership management solution. When the site is established, much of the procedure may be automated. This leaves the owner with a great source of passive revenue and the free time to continue planning ways to mature their business and their bottom line.

www.ingramcontent.com/pod-product-compliance
Lightning Source LLC
Chambersburg PA
CBHW030548220526
45463CB00007B/3028